My Soul's Desire

Meri Richardson, LSW, MHP, SPHR

Outskirts Press, Inc.
Denver, Colorado

Outskirts Press
http://www.outskirtspress.com

ISBN-13: 978-1-4327-0523-7

Library of Congress Control Number: 2007924930

Outskirts Press and the "OP" logo are trademarks belonging to
Outskirts Press, Inc.

Printed in the United States of America

Dedication

I would like to dedicate this book to the people who made it all possible—my birth mother, Svejora, who loved me enough to let me go; my adoptive mother, Edna, who loved me enough to find me; and to my son, Cade, whose love has helped me grow.

Special Thanks

I would also like to thank three special women in my life: Deb, who always believed in me; Karen, for opening the doorway to the eternal; and Sherry, for the ability to help my words come alive. I am blessed to be surrounded by such greatness.

Special thanks to Joseph who kept me focused and on track, which is no easy task.

Table of Contents

Introduction

What prompted me to write this book is not to forewarn you of the doom and gloom of adoption, but rather to offer up an alternative perspective of adoption—that of love, commitment, choice, growth, pain, and risk. Yes, there is pain and risk involved but that is where the growth comes from. I hope to offer both sides of adoption so you'll know what it feels like to adopt, and also to be an adopted child.

Let me begin by introducing myself. It is important that you know what knowledge and experience I bring to the adoption table. Describing me is a somewhat difficult task because I consider myself a multifaceted person depending on the time and day of the week and the role I may play at that time. First of which may be obvious, I am a woman. Furthermore, I am a Christian, wife, mother, daughter-in-law, sister-in-law, co-worker, social worker, infertile, forty-ish, adoptee, and adopter.

Now for my personality characteristics: I am headstrong, decisive, and focused thanks to my adopted father, hopeful, sensitive, and courageous thanks to my adopted mother. Unpredictable at times, thanks to hormones and, on occasion, fearful, ashamed, anxious, and angry thanks to being human. Thank goodness, these characteristics vary in their exhibition for if they didn't that would make the journey far too easy.

There may be many reasons why you have been drawn to this book. I can only assume that in some way you are connected to adoption either in thought or in experience. Maybe you were adopted yourself and would like to understand what that means for you personally. On the other hand, maybe you are wondering if you should adopt and need help with that process. Either way I feel compelled to tell you that this book is neither designed nor written as an instruction book. It will not contain a lot of statistics and/or generic information about adoption nor will you get a step-by-step detailed account of the administrative process you need to go through to adopt.

Please don't misunderstand me. I am not saying that type of information is not necessary or helpful—it is. However, what I want to focus on here is the emotional and psychological process of adoption and understanding or insight of what you bring to the table when adopting—a more important type of information. I believe adoption is personal and can only come from the heart, and so I intend for this book to be personal and from the heart. However, what you will get, I hope, is insight. Insight is extremely valuable, if not essential, to have when going through the adoption process. It's a quality we need to succeed in life. Insight can help you make wise and knowledgeable decisions that may affect your life. It then can give you the strength to live with those decisions.

You may ask, "Insight into what?" Well, insight into who *you* are and what *you* bring to the adoption table. This insight will help you also understand what others bring to the table—others who are being adopted, especially your own child.

It is also important to have insight into the women who have had the strength and integrity to give their children to others to rear. Whether a mother chooses to let her unborn child live or allows that child to have a new life with someone else, the insight gained from these women give you a different perspective on life. That is what adoption is, you know. It is life. I can guarantee you that adoption will change your thought processes and open your heart and mind. That is the great thing about adoption.

Adoption also brings the best and the worst out of us as we go through the process of living out our own adoption or the process of adopting another. Therefore, I believe it is important, no, *imperative* to be prepared as much as possible for the changes that occur in a person when they begin to think of adoption. Being unprepared can be devastating. Devastating in countless ways, not only to you but even more important the child or children involved as well. Adoption is not for the faint at heart, but more for the *lion* of heart.

Adoption <u>will</u> be emotionally challenging and if you are not prepared or willing to acknowledge and confront the emotional and psychological issues that arise through this process, it can lead to painful decision-making and possible traumatic outcomes.

So, as you can see, I take adoption very seriously. I think once you get into the book you will see why. Now that I have thoroughly preached and lectured, I can stumble off my soapbox with a clear conscience. My hope is that in reading my story, you will see similarities that will help you gain strength and understanding and insight.

I believe story telling is a wonderful way to edify, strengthen, and find connection with one another. Because this is my story, you will find me speaking bluntly and honestly about my thoughts and emotions growing up as an adopted child and what it was like to adopt a child of my own. I do this so you may know that you or your child is not abnormal but just human and that you are not alone.

So please join me in my journey of adoption. Laugh and cry along with me and experience one of the greatest gifts of all--*Life!*

If you cannot get rid of the family skeleton,
you may as well make it dance.

George Bernard Shaw

Chapter 1
My Story

My life's story is not one of high drama, but rather one filled with rich life experiences that have influenced and changed me over the years. I say this so you may begin to think about how your experiences have affected and influenced your daily life and decisions.

My story begins in a small village called Skjope, located in the former Yugoslavia near the border of Greece. In this village a young, pregnant, unmarried woman lived with her father. Times were hard in a community primarily known for farming and sheep-raising. Giving birth out of wedlock was not only a financial hardship but also a stigma to the family name. Therefore, with the urging of her father, she went to the adjoining village to give birth at an orphanage called the "Mothers Home." It was there she gave birth to me on August 14, 1960.

Born with black hair and olive skin, I held the characteristics of the culture of the people who resided in the surrounding villages. I am not sure whether it was my mother or the orphanage, but someone named me Meri. I lived at the orphanage for the first twenty-one months of my life until a family from the United States adopted me in May of 1962. What added even more intrigue to this adoption was that a major earthquake hit the area three months after I arrived in the United States. This earthquake destroyed the entire village and the orphanage where I was born.

A couple by the name of Edna and Alex Dimoff from Middletown, Pennsylvania, adopted me specifically because my adopted father's family hailed from the former Yugoslavia. In fact, he had family approximately two hours from the orphanage. Alex was first generation to be born in the states and was fortunate to have family members in that area aid with the adoption process.

Edna, my adopted mother, was unable to have children due to illness, so Alex asked his family from Yugoslavia to send pictures of children in the orphanage. The orphanage sent four pictures—two girls and two boys. When they looked at the pictures, Edna, thinking that Alex would like a boy, picked a boy but had picked out in her mind one of the little girls. Alex on the other hand had picked out a little girl but had not said anything yet to Edna. Now as it was told to me the conversation went something like this:

Alex asked Edna, "So which one do you want?"

Edna, being the good wife said, "I know you want a boy so how about this one?" Not being able to resist she added, "But isn't this little girl cute?" and Alex immediately said, "Okay, we'll get the girl."

Edna did not know that the girl she picked out was the very same little girl Alex picked out from the beginning. Needless to say they ended up with the little girl named Meri. (I did find out later that they wanted to name me Andrea Clay Dimoff but because I did not know English, and knew and responded to my name by that time, they decided to keep it Meri.) That is how I got to the United States of America. On May 28th 1962, I officially became Meri Andrea Dimoff and began my life in this small rural town of Middletown where I was raised as an only child. The aspect of being the only child became more significant in my life as I became older and I will talk more about that in a later chapter.

I grew up spoken to in my native tongue of Macedonian by my paternal grandmother. Spiritual customs of the Greek Orthodox Church and cultural rituals played a large part of my growing up. I always thought this was "neat" as a kid. None of my friends were bilingual nor had my ethnic look. It set me aside from the rest of my friends and made me feel special.

What I did not know was that in years to come these cultural differences would be not only an anchor for me but also a source of great loss. My grandmother who understood and spoke no English was my friend who kept my language alive until her death in 1975. At my young age of fifteen, this was my first experience with death. My father who also was bi-lingual but spoke only English to me because he felt, and stated to me on several occasions, that I was an American now and should speak English. So, after my grandmother's death it became more difficult for me to keep my native tongue, despite my best efforts to keep it alive. Can you believe I would actually hold a conversation with myself just so I could stay fluent? Believe me that made for some real boring conversations! But it also shows my commitment to keeping that part of my culture alive and how much I valued that part of myself.

My father was a very loyal American and a veteran of WW II, which I think, played a large part in his decision to not support me keeping my native tongue. Somehow, in his mind it seemed unpatriotic. He also was the patriarch, disciplinarian and decision-maker of the family as was customary of that period. However, I still regret the decision not to keep my language alive to this day. Macedonian was a strong part of my heritage and something I strongly identified with. It was also a dying language and very specific to my home region of Yugoslavia. Because it was so specific, teaching aids such as language tapes were unavailable. I tried the local Byzantine Churches and individual members from church who spoke the language but nobody knew how to get the information, especially since the war. Give this information some thought when adopting. If you adopt it will be important to have a firm knowledge of customs, traditions, and language so as to honor that part of your child's heritage and help in developing a sense of identity and belonging to the culture your child may come from. To lose that would be a great loss. It was for me.

As for my adoptive mother Edna, she was originally from Kentucky and a true southern belle. You should have heard her speak broken Macedonian with her southern accent. It was quite cute. The "Y'all" at the end of each statement added a bit of panache to the language as you might imagine. She kept that soft beautiful southern accent all her life.

She had a gentle and simple spirit about her but was the strength and backbone of our family. Edna brought balance to the household and kept it all together despite her continuous illnesses throughout her life. I grew up never knowing when or if my mother was going to die. What she ended up doing was teaching me about life and how your desire and love can keep you alive longer than any medicine or doctor.

3

That is quite a gift to be given. I thank her for that.

I grew up in the Dimoff household knowing I was adopted. I can't tell you when I actually knew, but there just didn't seem to be a time when I didn't know. I know there are probably several strains of thought on *when* you should tell your children they are adopted or *if* you should tell them.

I remember having a conversation with my husband Mike about this when we decided we were going to adopt. Mike did not think we should tell our adopted children. My first response was, "How can you not?" They would find out eventually and possibly feel betrayed. I did not want the child or children we would adopt to think there was anything to be ashamed of. Moreover, if we decided to wait until the right moment or when they are old enough to understand, well . . . when is that? And, old enough to understand what? I know I don't have an answer to those questions. I don't think you're ever too young to know that you are truly loved by not only your adoptive parents but also your birth parents who loved you enough to give you opportunities they could not provide. The details can come later when *they* want to know. Let the children tell you when and what they want to know.

I was pretty surprised I had such strong feelings about sharing our children's adoption with them and that I was so adamant about it. I guess because I grew up always knowing I was adopted and, since it was a very natural process and something to be celebrated, it just seemed like the only course to take.

I feel compelled to mention that if you do not want to tell your children they are adopted you should ask yourself some serious questions: Like why don't you want your children to know they are adopted? Is it because you are uncomfortable with the thought or is it because you do not want to deal with the questions and issues telling them will produce later on? Whatever the reason may be it is important to honestly answer those questions.

Another great event that most children my age did not have was the opportunity to experience what it was like to become a naturalized citizen of the United States of America. This was such a great experience. When I was eleven years old, my parents took me to the Lewisburg courthouse. As soon as we arrived, someone took me into a room and asked me questions such as who was the first president and current president—stuff like that. After that, they walked me into a different room and told me to pull my hair back away from my face. They took my picture and the black and white photo went on my certificate of Naturalization document. It was a horrific picture as you may have guessed and I still cringe when I look at it. Nevertheless, this is an extremely important document since my original birth certificate was destroyed in the earthquake at the orphanage.

After that, I stood before a judge alongside several adults (I was the only child present which felt strange) and pledged Allegiance to the United States of America. Then we raised our right hands and pledged our loyalty to the United States. The judge declared us officially United States citizens. That was a spectacular event for an eleven-year-old girl because not everyone can say they have done that. I think it is a shame you do not have to do that anymore. I believe now, once an international adoption is finalized, the children automatically become citizens of the United States. That was a special event for me and even today, having that certificate means a lot to me.

Growing up I thought it was special to be adopted. I would tell my friends that I was chosen by my family but my friends just happened. It wasn't till I got somewhat older, possibly my mid-teens, that I started rethinking this adoption thing. It seemed to hit me all of a sudden. I can't tell you exactly when but it suddenly occurred to me that to be adopted meant someone had to give me up and that someone was my mother. Adoption took on a completely new meaning.

It wasn't so neat for a while. I was going through adolescence and I started to feel rejected, thinking and wondering what I could have possibly done to cause my mother not to want me. As you may already know that is what children, do. If something significant happens in their lives, especially something negative, children are the first to take responsibility for the circumstances. You hear a lot about this in divorce situations. I think the same principle applies to adoption only on a more core level. Even though the initial thoughts and feelings may be the same, I believe there is a significant difference between the feelings generated from divorce and the feelings generated from adoption. These differences are at the very core of what it means to be an adopted child.

With divorce, most of the time at least one parent if not both parents are at least present or known by the child. In adoption, you may never know either parent. In divorce, a relationship existed between their parents that resulted in the birth of a child; therefore, the child is able to identify with why they are there. In other words there was an initial purpose for them being here. Many times in adoption the mother did not have a long standing committed relationship with the birth father and it becomes excruciatingly evident that the result of their birth was unplanned and unwanted. I am not sure how to explain it but there was something very significant to me about the fact that my mother was able to give birth to me and then able to choose to walk away knowing she would never see me again. That image was created and embedded in my mind. It left me feeling like there *must* have been something innately, horribly wrong with me to cause such an event. Mothers do not leave their children for no reason, right? Therefore, it must have been me. At that time, it just seemed to be the only explanation that made sense *in my mind*.

In my early adolescence, which is a tough time for children to begin with, feelings of abandonment and rejection began to accompany those thoughts. How those feelings played out was through anger, defiance, and depression. I wonder to this day, how my parents survived my teen-age years. I am sure they wondered the same thing. I think part of my anger and defiance was a testing ground to see if they were going to abandon me as well. My thoughts were, since my own mother did not want me why would these people stick it out. I thought I would just make it happen, that way I could be in control of how, when, and where I was going to be hurt or abandoned by them. Because *in my mind* being hurt and abandoned was inevitable. It was a turbulent time. It probably would have been even without being adopted, but I can say being adopted definitely added intensity to the already existing feelings of uncertainty about my very existence, development of my self-identity, and my self worth. (*Note: in the previous paragraph, I use the words* in my mind *a lot. Unfortunately, that is where it stayed and I will talk more about that.*)

It was shortly after all this started that I began asking a lot of questions. I wanted to know more about my birth parents, what the circumstances around my adoption were, and as stupid as it may sound, it was important for me to know who I looked like. I started looking through the adoption paperwork when my parents were not around to get some answers. Although there was little paperwork, all of the information I know today came from what my parents had. Moreover, what I told you about my adoption is all I know. My parents were not open in telling me what they knew. They would not even tell me they didn't know anything. I know it hurt their feelings that I wanted to know about my birth parents. I think my mother especially felt threatened and I know she thought that I wanted to know all this because I did not think of her as my mother, which was farthest from the truth. Please remember this is hindsight speaking, but I was young and just not able to communicate those feelings at the time. So, you do what you normally do when you can't communicate your feelings, you get angry.

I am telling you this because I think it is important to understand that children are not equipped to explain their feelings as intelligently as adults are. This only leads to frustration that leads to anger that in my case worked itself out in defiance and depression. However, if we as parents can recognize this and not take all the questions and feelings of abandonment personally it would help us to give our children the vocabulary and the room to discover and work out these feelings. It would also help us to discover that our children still consider us their parents and want us to be their parents throughout this whole process. (Sorry if that just sounded preachy but it's the social worker in me.) However, believe me, as a parent, having your child ask these types of questions is not emotionally easy process to walk through. It is extremely important that you are prepared.

As I entered young adulthood, the intensity of feeling rejected and abandoned subsided. A more accurate description is that my feelings just were filed away in a filing cabinet in the back of my mind. I found out that it never stays filed away, it just comes out later when life's circumstances pull the filing cabinet open again. Nevertheless, being busy with school and dating kept my mind otherwise occupied. What really helped was when, at twenty-eight years old, I went back to Yugoslavia with my father.

I was able to see the village I was born in, even if the orphanage and other original buildings were no longer there. I was able to speak freely in my native tongue, which came back quickly. I would even dream in Macedonian, which I thought was interesting. In addition, I was able to participate in the customs and lifestyle that accompanied this wonderful country. It truly was an unforgettable experience.

The only frustrating part about my visit was that again no one was willing to share with me any information regarding my birth mother or father. I got the distinct impression that my extended family members knew of my birth mother and were uncomfortable or unwilling to share any information about her. It was difficult to push the issue for fear of hurting my parents' feelings and causing everyone to feel uncomfortable. As mentioned before, I know that my mother's feelings would have been hurt if I continued to actively pursue looking for information about my birth mother. Ultimately, this kept me from ever being able to get any information. It was an emotional time for all of us. I think my father thought I was being ungrateful. I felt guilty, and both of my parents felt threatened. My mother finally shared with me when I was older that she thought if I found my birth mother that it would somehow change our relationship and that I would replace her with the new found mother. This was not even in my thoughts. I just wanted to know more about my birth mother and my circumstances.

At that period, it was important for me to know who I came from and where I came from. I had simple and insignificant questions like, "Where did I get my black curly hair and brown eyes? Is my personality like any of my birth parents? And how did I come to be?" I knew how, I mean "What were the circumstances surrounding my birth?" This strong desire to know lasted for most of my young adult life but began to fade over time. I guess I just moved on.

Despite all the questioning throughout this entire process I want to stress Edna and Alex Dimoff were and always will be my parents both in my mind and in my heart. However, because I could feel they were uncomfortable about talking about it, I did not take it further. However, it left me with a shroud of secrecy around my birth parents and me. And that left room for me to come up with my own assumptions. As you probably well know when left to our own devices what we can do to ourselves. I was my own worst enemy and of course, I assumed the worse. The secrecy only added to feelings of abandonment and then shame. I thought I must have had something to be ashamed of if they could not even talk about it.

Thoughts stampeded through my mind: "Was my mother raped? Did she have a fling? Was my father a cattle thief? A mass murderer? What was it that made it so awful to talk about it? That is what secrecy can do to you. This is why I am an advocate for telling children want they want to know or help them find the information. If you are not sure what is age-appropriate, trust me your children will tell you how much they want to know. I truly believe that it is not as important what you tell them but rather how and why. This brings me to a completely new topic of discussion.

Because we are human and do things motivated by our own feelings and insecurities, I think it is not only imperative but it is our primary responsibility as adoptive parents to find out as much information about the birth parents as possible. Get all the good, bad, and ugly. That way we can put it all in perspective for our children when they ask us questions and we can frame the information in a positive, loving way. I think it is important to share those good things about the birth parents to the child. Believe me it would be easy to tell them how awful the birth parents were so it looks like you saved them from a horrible fate. Then maybe they would be more grateful about you being their parent and eventually stop asking or better yet, not want to find their birth parents later. Who would want to find a birth-parent that was an addict and abandoned you on a street corner, right? WRONG! Do not be tempted to do it. You may say what kind of parent would do that, not me! Well you just wait until your child asks you the first question phrased just like this . . . "Mommy, what was my real mommy like?" Your stomach will knot up and you will be devastated. You will want to avoid the question or worse yet tell them all the gory details in order to persuade them you are the real mommy.

Look how my parents handled it—avoiding the situation with a smidgen of guilt for good measure. They were good parents, they meant well, and they wanted the best for me. That did not change how they handled it. So please do not do it. It does absolutely nothing for the child to hear that maybe their mother was a drug addict, young and in high school or ashamed of her pregnancy or had too many children and couldn't afford another child. Blah, blah, blah. All this does is devalue the child and confirm to them they were not wanted or worse yet think they were a charity case.

However, what is absolutely essential is for children to be able to have their own story of how they came to be where they are today. Moreover, this story should not be a horror story but a love story. Maybe their parent was a drug addict, so what? Those circumstances should not over shadow the fact that their birth mother chose to have them--made the commitment that their child's life was going to be better and had the desire for them to have a good and healthy life. Their birth mother wanted this so much that she was willing to sacrifice losing her child and endure the painful feelings of going through the adoption to assure that happened. That is magnificent stuff! That is a true *love story*.

On the other hand, maybe it is just telling your child all the good things, their strengths, talents or characteristics they have that make them special. Whatever it is, that is crucial and critical information that adds value to the child.

Also, the more we know of the parent the more credible we become in sharing that information with our children and the more it means to them and adds to the love story of their life. Have I preached enough about this yet?

Now, let us move on with my story. As I got closer to thirty I wanted to start building permanent relationships. It's that time in your life when you wake up and look at your parents and they have suddenly become old people. You're not quite sure how and where you were when it happened you realize your parents are not the youthful people you remember them to be. Their mortality becomes suddenly obvious and so does your own. You also have become the older person you remember thinking you would never become. Life has this way of circling around and biting you in the butt when you're busy looking in the other direction. This is also the time where you begin to understand the value of having parents and the importance of family because you are at the point in your life where you want your own family.

As my parents got older, I was feeling the need for stability and permanence. Now some of this was just a natural stage of my development that occurs as you mature. However, it was slightly different, or at least it felt like it was. I believe adoption placed a different emphasis on my need for family and permanence. The word that comes to mind to describe that difference is "intensity." The need to connect to others was becoming increasingly urgent. Note the word *urgent* used here. This is where I began to really wish I had at least a brother or sister. There was a real sudden awareness of a loss of not having a brother or sister. Panic would be an appropriate word here too. I was beginning to understand that my parents would not be around forever, that left only me, and it was coming to the forefront rather quickly. I just did not know it was going to happen as quickly as it did.

The coming events in my life were probably the most significant, painful, and enlightening, and have had the most influence in shaping me today. Being adopted is what added the significance to this situation. As mentioned before I was the only child and, due to family dynamics, not very close to other relatives. You may wonder what the family dynamics were: well, at times it felt that my extended family— aunts and uncles—did not quite accept me as an integrated part of the family because I was not a "blood" relative. I do not have many specifics to give you other than that was just how it felt.

Christmas was a time when those feelings seemed most prevalent. Because my extended family did not know me very well I would get gifts that were not personalized to my interests or likes. Not to mention, I was not included in much of the conversation. My dad and uncle would speak Macedonian to each other but not to me. I would try to listen and understand their conversation but over the years it got harder and harder and they seemed to talk faster and faster. I am not blaming anyone here; that was just the way I felt. I am sure my extended family did not want me to feel that way. Nor did they know I felt that way. There were factors that added to these dynamics: I was the youngest in the entire family. My youngest cousin was approximately 15 years older than I. It felt like they were just going through the motions of including me the best they could. In addition, it was also the era of children being seen and not heard. Try that mentality today! My children would not stand for that for one minute and they are four and five. But, I am glad for it.

Then it happen. I was thirty-one in 1991 when my father died suddenly from cancer. By suddenly I mean diagnosed in May and gone in July. In 1992, my maternal grandmother died and in 1993, my mother died of a heart attack. However, I truly believe my mother died of a broken heart after losing my father. Unfortunately, there is no medical treatment for a broken heart.

I can remember coming home from the hospital as if it was yesterday after my mother died. The first thing I did was go to my bed, curl up, and became engulfed in intense feelings of abandonment. The first thought that came to my mind upon hitting the bed was, *"I am an orphan again"* I don't belong to anyone anymore. I will never be Alex or Edna's daughter again.

As I write this, I can still feel the feeling of being lost and alone. What I just told you is what adoption brings to the table each time

11

there is a loss. That is why I think it is important to have siblings. That there is someone connected to you that knew you and grew up with you. Even though I had close, long-time friends, it was not the same as family. It is hard to explain. But, there is something very significant about having someone in your life that you have identified with since early childhood. Someone who has a history of life experiences with you from the very beginning—both the good and the bad it really does not matter.

This was especially critical since I did not know anything about my biological family. Essentially my life began with my adoptive parents at that age of two. Once my parents died that was all gone. My history was gone. The person I knew who was always someone's daughter was now no one's daughter and I never was and never will be someone's sister.

To add insult to injury there was a war waging right in my family's back yard in Yugoslavia. I did not even have a country that I would recognize anymore let alone visit. That is big stuff to feel and experience. I still can feel the loss especially around the holidays. The intensity of the feelings was overwhelming at times.

So, what is the first thing you want to do when you are in pain? You want to get out of it any way you can. Well the first thing I felt driven to do was to create my own family. Now remember the word *intensity* here. It is a key word. Remember when I said we make decisions based on our emotions. I am no exception to that rule (all the degrees in the world don't keep you from that). The intensity of grief, loss, fear, and feeling s of being disconnected drove me to my next decision. I made a bad relationship choice that resulted in a brief marriage that ended in divorce. At the time the *intensity* and *urgency* to connect and belong "somewhere" was clouding my judgment.

However, I have to say I acquired my father's strong will and determination and was able to get out of it quickly and move forward. I acquired my father's tenacity. I truly believe no matter what age our children are we can offer them our good qualities that will stay with them and help them through the tough times. (A side note there—after the divorce I set out on a mission to redefine myself, which needed to be done anyway. I took time to reassess my life and develop my spirituality, which helped me to see the big picture)

Once I did that I met my current husband Mike, which brings me to a new phase of my life.

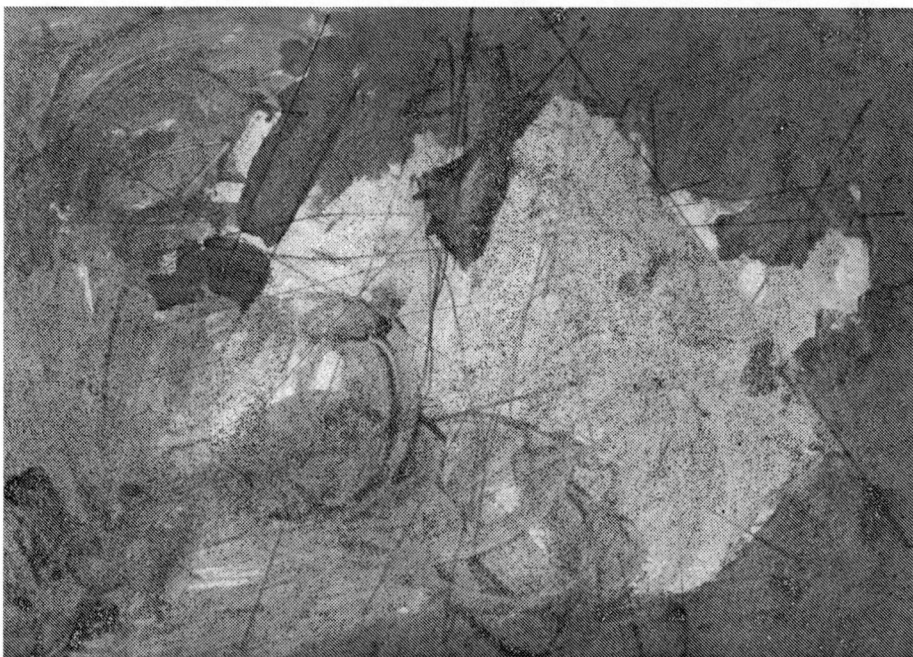

The only cure for grief is action.

George Henry Lewes

Chapter 2
Infertility

Well if it is not one thing, it's another. Life has a way of constantly keeping you on your toes. Once Mike and I settled in, we wanted to start a family as soon as we could. I was thirty-nine when we got married and we tried to have a baby of our own immediately. The old biological clock was ticking-- well maybe it had stopped—I just didn't know it at the time.

After two years of me crying every time I saw a pregnant woman or small child we started to look at adoption. I was lucky. Mike was open to adoption from the very beginning. And I certainly was based on my history. Therefore, we began the process of adoption and put aside trying to have a biological family.

Now what was interesting was that once we decided to adopt I felt very strongly about not getting pregnant. I felt that if I continued trying to get pregnant it would somehow negate or take away from the adoption process and the prospective child. I did not want our adopted child to feel like he or she was a second choice or a back up plan. It almost felt like I was devaluing our prospective child. I also wanted to focus on preparing to bring a child into our family. I could not do that and go through the emotional part of trying to have a child at the same time.

Even though we felt like it was the right decision it did not make it an easy one. It was yet another loss for me. I would look at pregnant women and wonder what was wrong with me that I could not have a child. I would ask God what I did that was so wrong that He would punish me like this? I finally met a wonderful man and we would make wonderful parents—why now? I was angry and feeling less than a woman, as each day passed. I was angry that I was starting a phase of my life that others started in their late twenties. I felt like I lost twenty years of my life.

I felt behind the rest of the world. I was beginning to feel old for the first time in my life. In addition, to having the medical profession constantly reminding me on a daily basis that you are *way past* the childbearing period didn't help the situation. I was angry that they would just look at my age. Note, I said "age." They did not bother to look up at me or see me as a person. They would just write me off and tell me, "You only have one option" then give me percentages of success that match my shoe size.

After the doctors gave us the grim statistics, and I hate statistics, they would tell us it was only going to cost $8,000 to try to get pregnant and they most graciously offered to throw in a good case of insanity, depression, and mood swings as a bonus just for giving the process a try. I apologize for the sarcasm. What am I saying? No, I don't.

I think the medical profession could use some pointers in handling this area of medicine a little better. I had a hard time understanding all of it. I felt healthy. I just completed a marathon, was biking and exercising, and felt good. I didn't feel unhealthy nor did I feel old till everyone began telling me I was. It was not a good time of my life. But most learning experiences aren't. It definitely was an emotional time for me. However, time has a way of giving you distance from the pain. What you do with that time and distance is what heals or hurts you. Time only allows you to make decisions good or bad. I had to take responsibility for how I viewed both this situation and myself. I had to ask myself: Do I want to define my self worth solely by one aspect of my life? And what was more important to me: Giving birth or having a family? I decided that having a family and being a mother far exceeded my need and desire to experience a healthy pregnancy. Pregnancy and motherhood were not synonymous.

Please read this again: Pregnancy and motherhood is not the same thing. This helped me refocus on what was important. It was not easy **and** it is a process. Nevertheless, it's important to be objective and see things from a clear mind and heart. Only then can we begin to see the doors, windows begin to open, and *your* "Souls Desire" come to life.

I look back now and I do not feel the loss of never having experienced pregnancy and giving birth. It's just not important as it once was. If I could say one thing to women who struggle with this issue it would be this: "Yes, you can still be a mother no matter what your circumstances if that is your desire. Just open your heart to the possibilities."

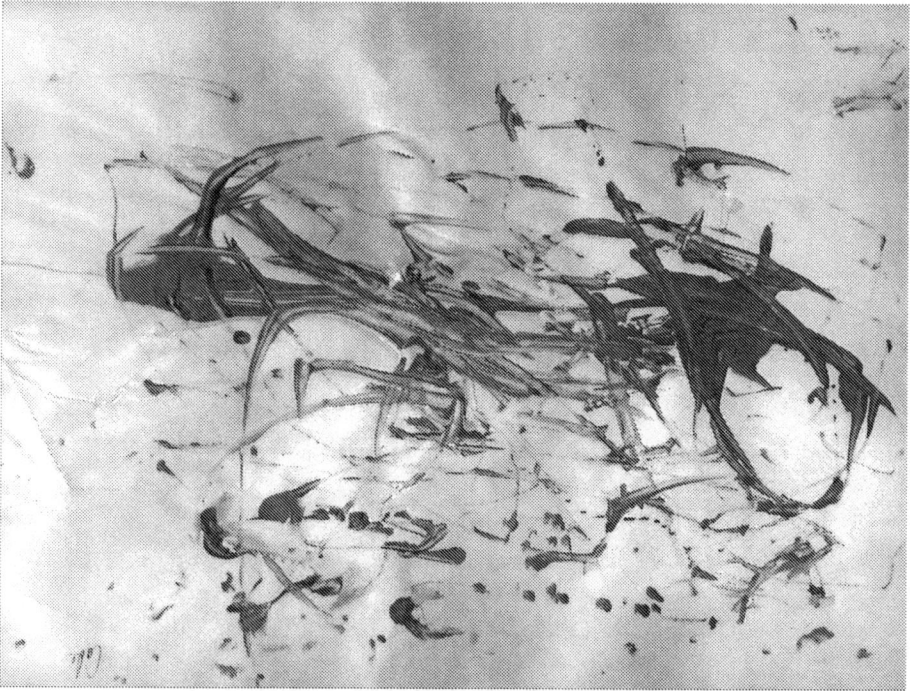

Life engenders life. Energy creates energy. It is by spending one-self that one becomes rich.

Sara Bernhardt

Chapter 3
We Chose Life

Mike and I came to the conclusion early that we would choose life whether we created it ourselves or whether it was created for us by another. So we began to put our energy into searching for our child.

I will never forget when Mike and I went to the adoption agency for the first time. We met with a caseworker, Lori, who was obviously pregnant with her third child. In my mind I was thinking how audacious! I remember not liking her immediately and thinking what does she know about not being able to have children? How can she help us? Now remember, our actions are based on our thoughts and emotions. My illogical thoughts were running amok. Her being pregnant did not have anything to do with being competent. And competent she was! We were not there for her to help us with our infertility but rather for her to help us with adopting a child. There is a difference, you know? It just took me a few days to figure that one out. Lori knows all this now because we were able to talk about it. I make a point of telling you this because it is **extremely** important that you deal with these issues up front and get them out of the way. If I hadn't dealt with the issue it could have kept us from staying with the agency and using their services. Mike and I would have lost the opportunity and blessing of having Cade with us today. So after talking with her about my feelings it did pass and I have grown to respect Lori. It was one of the many issues that I needed to work through and she helped me do that just by being pregnant and open to discussion. Well once again all things happen for a reason. If only we would look at difficult situations and ask ourselves, "What am I to learn from this?" If we did so, painful situations wouldn't last as long. However, that's just my opinion of life.

Lori forced me to deal with my feelings about not being able to get pregnant and to finally put it all in perspective. However, I do know if I had not dealt with my feelings they would have filtered down to our son. I think it would have given him the message that he was second best since we couldn't get pregnant. I don't know that for sure, it's not a scientific statement. It's just that I felt I had to resolve it. I didn't want to take that chance of my anger and disappointment affecting my ability to love our child. I didn't want to continue to feel angry about it either. The whole thing was just getting old and tiring me out.

So once we sorted it all out we began the adoption process. The one thing that I don't think you can prepare yourself for is the constant bombardment of children for adoption. I would get on the Internet and felt I could be there for weeks and not see all the children that needed a home. I would get angry with God and say, "How can you let all these children stay orphans? What is the purpose of all this?" The reasons for adoption—abuse, neglect, abandonment—were hard to read about. There is a story for each child's face on the Internet, which means all of them are in the system for a particular reason and the reason is definitely not a pleasant one. And that's not including all the perspective birth mothers out there on the Internet as well. Add to that the costs, legal technicalities, and paperwork and it makes for a very trying emotional time. Mike and I would get a little miffed knowing we would make great parents. So why did we have to prove ourselves? Can you visualize me stomping my feet in the middle of the living room saying, "That's not fair! They should be giving us children!" Didn't I say adoption brings out the best and worst of us?

Then there were also times where we felt like we were paying for or buying children like they were some sort of commodity. Of course, like any commodity, certain children would cost more than other children. Then to top it all off certain agencies would only handle certain situations and charge you your life's savings, not to mention years of waiting. I found this all unbelievable. It made us angry. We were past miffed. But that is just the way it was and is. The old supply and demand rule applies to everything it seems, even a life. But that's another issue and possibly another book.

The point to be made with all of this is, it is important to work with a good agency. Emotions can run rampant causing you to make decisions you might not normally make if you were able to keep things in perspective. You might miss a wonderful opportunity for a beautiful child, something you would regret the rest of your life. Once we got past the frustration and were able to understand the reasoning behind what needed to be done, we were able to continue to move forward. Note I did not say "agree" but "understand." Understanding can help you to see the importance of doing it right so that you don't become one of the cases that turn into a horror story and end up on Sixty Minutes. You don't hear about the other ones that turn out beautifully. Please keep that in mind when you hear those stories. You see, sometimes staying focused on all the problems of the system and injustices of the world can be a great smoke screen for not confronting your own personal unresolved feelings. Everyone has unresolved feelings. You wouldn't be alive this long to not have any, you just may not know what they are . . . yet. But you have to be prepared to deal with your own feelings because they will be triggered once you start this process.

You will always be dealing with some type of feeling during the adoption process. And in this particular situation I have to admit I was doing just that. I had to resolve the feelings of despair and hopelessness I was feeling for these children and get over the idea that I couldn't help them all. I was tapping into my own feelings of abandonment and thoughts of "that's me." I could relate to every face I saw. Finally, I had to stop looking. This is where my faith, combined with an understanding of the system, helped me. My faith told me that God has a plan for each and every one of those little faces and guess what—it wasn't me.

By understanding the system I understood how it was designed to hopefully secure families for these children. There was also another little tidbit that came to mind—that people working within the system make a difference. Make sure you know and understand the ethics, belief system, and services of the adoption agency you are considering. I am very sorry to say that not all agencies take the high road when dealing with adoption. *So it is important to find an agency operating with integrity and working for the **child's best interest first**, not yours,* *and that they are focused.* Should I say that again? Because there is a significant point here—just because Mike and I were going to this agency and paying them for their services, I wanted an agency that had a focus of providing what was best for the child—even if that meant being brutally honest with the birthparents and me. I wanted the child to be the center. Maybe my focus was different because I was adopted and I didn't believe I had someone advocating or looking out for me other than God. I wanted the child that was ultimately ours to know he or she was our first priority from the very beginning.

To give you an example on how we make decisions from our emotions and the importance of a supportive agency is when Lori presented us with a prospective mother. It turns out she happened to be our son Cade's birth mother. I had a knee jerk reaction of, "no way!" Now think about it. This is coming from someone who just went through wanting a child, worked through her own infertility, and desperately wanted a family. It goes to show you how intense your emotions can be during the process and the illogical thoughts and feelings that it can produce. It's important to allow time to process the information you get. Here was the situation: The birth mother was in jail, didn't know who the father might be—I mean, really didn't know—and had used drugs during the first trimester. My first reaction was to judge the mother by her life style, vocalize anger that she would jeopardize a life, be so careless, irresponsible, selfish, blah, blah, blah, on and on. As a social worker, I dealt with situations like this for years and all of a sudden I got self-righteous—like I had that right. The feelings and thoughts were so abrupt that it surprised me and embarrassed me all at the same time. Which, I might add, was a good thing—a very good thing. It brought me back to reality and made me feel ashamed of myself, which was appropriate and well deserved.

I feel compelled to remind you that I have over 20 years experience in the mental health field. It has come in handy in recognizing what is going on emotionally with me. Again, all the education in the world does not exempt you from being human and feeling and thinking these things. It just gives you more tools to get through it. So, someone who does not have that background really needs to rely on the agency to help them through this process. You just have to be willing to talk about your thoughts and your emotions openly.

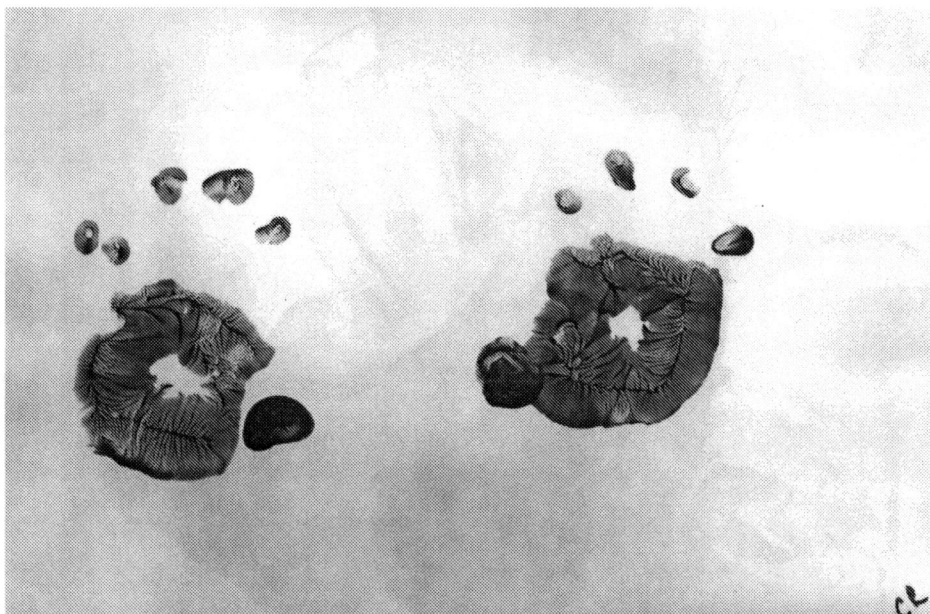

Love is everything it's cracked up to be . . . . It really is worth fighting for, being brave for, risking everything for.

Erica Jong

Chapter 4
A Mother's Love

O nce I got off my high horse and was able to think more clearly, Mike and I agreed to meet with Cade's birth mother Monica. We found her to be very personable and caring about her unborn son. In fact, we keep in contact with pictures and letters and occasionally meet to this day. This brings me to an issue that all adoptive parents must decide: How much, if any, contact do you keep with the birth mother? I really believe that each situation will be different and warrant a decision based on the situation and those decisions can change with time and the circumstances. I guess I bring it up because your first reaction may be as ours was—"absolutely none." I hope that you would be open to at least looking at all the possible means of communication if the birthmother requests it.

Believe me, I know the first thing that goes through your mind. It went through mine. "You're the one who's giving him up and I want to be the parent not you." That came from my fear of the child not thinking of me as his mother. Does that sound familiar? Now I know how my mother felt! I mean we should work for the benefit of the child which is the ultimate goal, isn't it? I know I initially had thoughts along that line before we even knew about Cade's mother. I thought that I wouldn't want any contact or even meet the birth mother but I am grateful that I changed my mind. This is just yet another example of why it is so important to work through those feelings. Tired of me telling you that yet? If you are, it's a good sign that you're starting to actually understand emotionally and not just intellectually.

In my specific case I was able to see first hand how much she wanted a good home for her son and to provide him with something she could not—stability, two parents, and a home. She didn't want foster care; she wanted permanence for him even if it meant that she left him forever. Now remember me talking about the importance of having a love story to tell? This is a prime example. By meeting Cade's mother I was able to acquire important information for me to share with Cade as he grows up.

You remember how uncertain things were with my own adoption? I knew very little about my birth parents. As I mentioned before it almost seemed as though there was a circle of shame or secrecy around my birth. I believe I could have benefited from knowing about my birth parents. I want Cade to know about his birth mother. I want him to know that the circumstances of her life may have been a contributing factor in placing him for adoption but it was her great love for him that caused her to be steadfast in her decision. You can never have too many people who love you. It will help Cade when he starts to ask the same questions I did. How could my mom leave me? I can tell him a beautiful love story that is all his own and will help in his understanding and healing. That was something I did not have. I will be able to say first hand that I met her and tell him what she was like. Cade's birth mother has written letters to him and has given him gifts all of which I keep. I have laminated the letters for safekeeping and I will share them with him when he gets older. I want him to have something tangible that he can look at to remind him that he is loved. And you know what? The thought of sharing those letters and things with him doesn't scare me in the least. If he wants to spend time with his birth-mother when he gets older that thought doesn't scare me either. If you get the sense that I'm full of BS, you're right. But I hope I'm adult enough to respond to him in a positive and healthy manner. It will cause me heartache when he first brings it up—I'm only human.

My security lies in the fact that I will have years of joy, years of pain, years of strong relationship building, and years of loving him unconditionally under my belt. This will give me the strength I need to support him in whatever direction he wants to go. And I will make a point of doing this for only one reason—*I* am his mother.

So, I am hoping you can see the importance of obtaining as much information about the birthparents as you can. And meeting them if at all possible and appropriate, no matter how difficult it may be for you to do. Think about this a little more. We meet this woman who is giving birth and has decided that she wants us to be her son's parents. It doesn't hit you in the beginning but you do come to realize what a great and wonderful compliment that gift is. A woman is offering her child to you. Not just for a week but forever. Sit with that thought and see if it isn't a humbling feeling.

Then all of a sudden a fire blazed in my mind and my emotions ran wild. It was time to prepare for Cade's arrival. I found myself beginning to nest. Cross stitching booties and making a baby blanket. Thoughts of a child are all-consuming—at least it was for me. Mike, on the other hand, was a little different. He would go from trying to be detached to getting excited. He tried not to get too excited due to the fear that the birth mother might change her mind.

One evening while at the dinner table he said out of the blue that we shouldn't get our hopes up about this child or get too emotionally attached because a lot could happen. We both knew that was true. But then in the same breath he said, "What do you think about the name Cade?" I'm looking at him like don't get attached huh. But I thought it was great and it took all of 10 seconds to come to an agreement of his name. Actually, Mike had given it much thought. Cade was named after a rancher in Montana that Mike knew. He wanted to share his love and respect for nature, wildlife and his yearning for the simple life of the west . That was his way of sharing that part of him with his son. And that is how Cade got his name. Well, once I had a name I started to think about what I wanted Cade to have from the very moment of his life. Now notice that the trying not to get too excited or attached just flew right out the window.

I have come to believe when you adopt, you have to be willing to get emotionally attached from the first moment you begin the adoption process. You first get attached to the prospect of a child then to a real life child. But no doubt about it, it's a risk—a risk I think is worthwhile even if you have to go through a long process several times till the adoption is actually finalized. We accepted Cade as "our" child even before he was born. We had the option of placing Cade into foster care until finalization but we didn't want that for "our" child. We wanted to take the risk, to offer him the love we had from the very beginning of his life even if it meant giving him back.

Don't get me wrong, it would have killed us to give him back but at least we could say we loved him and cared for him until that day and the blessing of having him for that time would had been worth it. We could honestly say that we held up our end of the commitment to Cade. We would have the security of knowing that he was being loved and cared for during that time. If we hadn't taken that risk, we would have lost six months of bonding time and joy that we could never recoup. I guess playing it safe has never been the path I opted for. I started to ask myself questions like, "What didn't I have that I want Cade to have?" "What was important?"

Well what I wanted for Cade was for him to have his own story and to offer him the knowledge that he was wanted and that we wanted him specifically before he was born. He will know that although he was not planned for he was wanted and loved by two mothers and a father. I think being wanted is much more important than being planned for. So, I started a journal. I started with a little history of both of families. I then wrote about how Mike and I met, wanted a family, how God presented us with Cade, and his birth mother being the angel God sent us. I wrote how we started to plan and prepare for him even before we knew of his existence, how we grew to love him and talked about him every waking moment before he arrived and explained to him how he got his name and what our dreams and aspirations were for him.

I wanted to give his life a purpose. I wanted him to have an understanding about the divine nature that caused him to be here now, in this place, and at this time, and see the larger picture of his life. I wanted him to actually see and know that there is a plan for him even if we do not always know what that plan is, and to know that plan is designed out of love for him. I guess I wanted a lot for him. That is what makes a parent. So I went about trying to provide that for him. I have a box where I keep all his keepsakes, pictures of baby showers that were held in his honor and letters, his drawings, and this book.

I believe in looking reality straight in the eye and denying it.

Garrison Keillor.

Chapter 5
Entering the "Zone"

When I refer to the "Zone," I am not referring to the food we eat or the type of exercise we do. This is far beyond that place. I'm referring to the place where our surroundings sometimes become blurred, time purposely slows down or speeds up at a whim and all that was important the minute before you got *the call* has no meaning anymore. That's what I mean about the "Zone."

Well I remember getting *the call*. Lori called us from the hospital to tell us that Cade was about to be born and asked the million-dollar question: "How soon can you get to the hospital?" Too bad Scotty wasn't around to beam us up! I was at work and I knew all my surrounding co-workers knew when Cade was born by the loud, "*NOW*" that came out of my office. I called Mike and asked if he was ready to be a father yet, because if he wasn't he better get with it and get with it quick! We ended up at the hospital five hours after he was born. My heart was in my throat. My mind was racing, because I couldn't keep up with all the facts. I remember walking into the hospital and the closer we got to the maternity floor the more anxious I got.

We got to the maternity ward and at the end of the hallway was Lori. Once she saw us, she started to wheel the cart Cade was lying in down the hallway. I felt like I was under water. Everything was slow motion and in my mind I kept thinking, "Okay, old woman, this is the moment you have been waiting for all your life. It may have come later than you wanted but it's here now. Don't miss a single second of it."

I had to fight to keep my mind in the present. He finally got to us which seemed to take forever and we looked in the cart and my initial thoughts were "are you sure he's in there?" I didn't see anything but a small white blanket that was rolled up to look like a cocoon. He was so tiny that we could not see him until Lori moved the blanket. And there he was, this perfect tiny little face peeping out. He was born at 11:25 a.m. and we took our first look at him at 4:30 p.m. He weighed 6 pounds, 14 ounces. He was just a little peanut. We immediately took him to the nursery where we could hold him and feed him. I remember wondering who would hold him first. I wanted to take him and run home with him but knew I couldn't. I picked him up and thought Mike should be the first to hold him. I knew Mike wanted a boy and thought it only right for him to hold him first. I thought Mike might refuse because he was so small. However, Mike just reached out his arms and took him as if it was the most natural thing in the world. Of course, we were taking pictures and trying to hold on to the moment the best we could. Then the nurse came in and said we could feed him. Mike handed Cade to me and I gave him his first meal. He ate like a champion and still does till this day, I might add.

The only problem I had was that the hospital staff referred to him as baby boy _____ (birth mother's last name) like he was abandoned on some doorstep and was a John Doe not belonging to anyone. I felt like telling them he had a first name and it's Cade, and his last name is Richardson and don't you forget it. I guess I was a little sensitive. However, I knew it was just a temporary situation. It did not stop me from asking the nurse to put his first name on the chart for me. He was ours, no doubt about it. It was hard leaving him that evening. However, as with all good blessings, Cade was kind enough to be born on a Friday so we came the next day and brought the family. His grandmother and aunt came with us. The hospital gave us an empty room to visit with Cade since we would not be able to take him home until Sunday. We all took turns holding him and his grandma and aunt took turns crying. We wore Cade out and he finally fell asleep on his daddy's chest, which seemed like the only place on earth he belonged.

Well, the day had arrived. It was Sunday morning, May 13th and Mothers Day. How cool was that? I woke up and thought this is really happening—I can't believe it. We could take him home with us. He's ours. Now up to this point I was able to remain calm, cool, and collected, even though the knot in my stomach and throat was big enough to choke a rhino. I just had not allowed myself to cry yet. Not sure why, but I knew it was going to happen eventually. We hurried around and made sure we had a full diaper bag with his first clothes, diapers, bottles, and a car seat. We got to the hospital around noon. I walked through the hospital, trying not to run full speed to the maternity ward.

Want to hear something crazy? I felt compelled to stop in the bathroom to make sure I was presentable. I wanted to make a good impression. Isn't that weird? As if he was going to remember what I looked like or stand up and say I don't think I want you as my mommy, you're not pretty enough. Well, after the pit stop we finally got to the unit. Monica had already left. The nurse came over and gave us bags with all kinds of stuff—food, magazines, diaper bag—and then showed us how to bathe him. We gave Cade a bath and dressed him in his new clothes, which were, of course, too big for him. Then they asked if we wanted pictures taken of him. Well certainly! We wanted this moment to last forever. So, they took a few pictures. We ordered about 1000 too many, which I understand is a ritual that must take place before you take your child home. It just is not the same if you do not have about 989 pictures too many and have to go through the phone book to find addresses in which to send all the pictures. I might add I had the initial urge to do just that! He was our precious baby and I wanted the world to know.

After the picture taking was over it was time to go. It was not until I got to the elevator where Mike, Cade, the nurse, and I were waiting that it hit me. I say "it" because there would be no words to describe what "it" was. All I knew was that I couldn't stop it. I started to cry thinking, "Oh my God, this tiny little being is coming home with us. I am a mother starting today!" Did I tell you it was Mothers Day? Sorry, I had to rub it in one more time! As of this moment, I began being Cade's mother and he was going to know me as his mother for the rest of my life! I now have a son! It was overwhelming to say the least.

By the time we got to the car, I was able to pull myself together. I wanted to hold him but knew he needed to go in the backseat where I sat next to him. I had put a little sign up in the back window that said, "Baby on Board". I wanted the whole world to know we had a son. Before leaving home, we placed a sign in the front of the house saying new arrival with his name on it and balloons attached. We got home and the family all showed up. We passed him around, held him, and celebrated in his arrival. We all then went out to eat at a local restaurant where everyone knew us and we showed him off even more. He has been a traveler ever since.

However, one of the most important and memorable trips we took was to the courthouse to finalize the adoption. This is where the courts finally catch up with what is in your heart, and what God had already accepted, that this child, Cade, was to be a permanent member of our family. The courts would finally acknowledge us as his parents.

It can be very overwhelming to go into a large courtroom, but we had a wonderful and caring judge. That is not always the case. But there is something very special about going before a judge and raising your hand to the heavens, pledging to accept full responsibility to love and care for your child for the rest of your life. It was an emotional and heartfelt experience all parents should go through. I walked out of the courthouse a changed person. I walked in self-absorbed and selfish. Most of my life was spent thinking and taking care of myself. But everything changed because love and commitment has transformed me into this selfless person with a higher mission in life. This higher mission gave me a new identity—"a mommy" who has just pledged to love and care for a child for the rest of his life. I will never be the same again.

This takes us to today. As of January 2007, Cade is five years old and is growing up fat and sassy just like his mother.

Now that you have Cade's and my adoption story, I would like to talk a little more about how my own adoption has influenced my adult life. In addition, how being adopted has added a new dimension and understanding to my life as well as how adopting children has actually aided in my own personal healing.

We don't receive wisdom, we must discover it for ourselves after a journey that no one can take for us or spare us.

Marcel Proust

Chapter 6
Looking Through the Eyes of Adoption

I do not want you to think that every trial and conflict in my life is related to, or caused by, being adopted. Believe me; I do not think that is true by any stretch of the imagination. However, being adopted does affect certain aspects of my life because it is apart of who I am.

There will be times in your life, as well, that you will acknowledge the same truth; when you will be reminded that certain aspects of your life have defined who you are. Being adopted is certainly one of those circumstances that at times set's you apart from the rest. When you go to the doctor they ask your family history. If you have been adopted, you may not have that information.

Or maybe, like me, you don't have a birth certificate but rather a naturalization certificate. If needed for employment or passport, it's just another explanation you must make to verify who you are. Most of the time, you must justify your situation when you least expect it.

However, adoption has offered me great gifts as well. Here are just a few of those gifts: I believe I have a greater appreciation for family and, more importantly, that family is not limited to bloodlines but by choice and love. It has helped me see the divine nature of my life—that there was someone out there who had a loving plan for me and was watching out for me. This has helped me through many tough times and continues to do so today.

Being adopted has also challenged me to define myself. I do not believe most people think about this. Because I didn't know where my characteristics came from, i.e. mother, father, genetic factor, as I got older, it was easier for me to choose which way I wanted to be. For example, in the beginning of the book I describe myself personally. Those characteristics were developed by choice. I never felt hindered by genetics or felt helpless to change anything because I was tied to a set of DNA. I have acquired many characteristics of my adoptive parents, but I never felt hindered by those characteristics. There was the sense of freedom to change whatever I wanted about myself because there was no identification to genetics or DNA.

I guess to state it simply—it is much easier to change your mind than your genes.

I know with certainty that being adopted has affected my ability to connect with others. And I think that my personal circumstances of being in an orphanage for twenty-one months have contributed to this. Even though I feel a strong bond with my friends and family there is always just a little piece of me I know I set aside. It is a vague awareness that I am not sure is either good or bad now. I remember thinking and feeling this as a child and feeling frustrated because of it. It added to my feelings of loneliness and made me a little scared. I was scared of the thought that I would always remain separate and apart from the rest of the world even if I did not want to.

I am still aware of those feelings today but it is just that— awareness. However, the good news is I realized that as an adult I could make choices—choices about relationships. I could choose whom I wanted to relate to and what type of relationship I wanted to enter into. So with knowledge and understanding of relationship building and my part as a builder, I have been able to have long-standing, positive relationships with the people I choose.

As I found in life, good can come out of unhappy circumstances and the ability to separate myself has, to some degree, assisted me in my field. It has allowed me to remain objective when helping others, yet allowed me to pull from my life experiences. It is the best of both worlds. It all comes down to self-responsibility and self-realization. Being adopted has affected both my relationships and my decision-making. It has helped in creating the positive, healthy life perspective I have today.

As I look back on my life, I realized that adoption had a role in my emotional attachments. I found I did not rely on others to take care of me, even though I spent much of my time wishing someone would. How is that for a paradox? I desperately wanted someone to take care of me but I would not trust anyone to do it. "I can do it myself" is the phrase I always would fall back on. The fear of experiencing the pain of being abandoned was far too great a risk to take, at least in my mind.

Years later I realized I had choices on how I could handle those fears of disconnectedness and being self-reliant. Therefore, what I did is to come up with a game plan. To help fight my feelings of separation I stayed connected to my current family and my adopted parents with family traditions and rituals. I made a conscious effort to keep my childhood family traditions in my present family. I also came to discover that the holidays were a time of grieving the loss of my family—it is for many people because home is where family traditions were most present. There is always this thought in the back of my mind that I know how much Mom and Dad would love to see Cade and be with us for the holidays. One thing my parents stressed was the importance of having family around during the holidays no matter how old I got, even if it was only Mom, Dad, the dog and I. To combat my feelings of sadness over the loss of my parents I brought my childhood traditions and rituals into my current family. I make Baklava and Peta each year the way my mom taught me. This brings her into my home for the holidays. Family rituals allow us to bring those who have gone, back into our lives through remembrance.

Our family was unique. My Kentucky-raised mother was taught by her non-English speaking mother-in law to make Baklava and other ethnic treats. She, in turn, taught her daughter and I will teach mine. This was the way we prepared for Christmas each year. I grew up with the smells of Greek pastries permeating the home. It signaled that Santa was coming and soon! (By the way here's a hint for this Christmas year. I know Santa's favorite food is Baklava because he always cleaned his plate each year and left me great gifts.) I now bring that tradition to my family. (Santa still cleans his plate and leaves great gifts so it must be working.)

This keeping of tradition helps me heal and remember each year and helps keep me bonded to my parents in spirit. But it does even more than that—it honors them and the gifts they left me. Traditions or rituals are one of those things that add value to your family and will add warmth to your child's love story. It will help your family bond and develop a sense of unity—a vital survival strategy of the family structure. I also think it important to mention that I was not aware of all this significance until I got married. Funny how getting married can bring all this to light.

There is another relationship that I have not talked about yet, and I think it's important to mention. That is my relationship with God. Just when I think I have all the answers, I realize that I do not even know what the question is. Just when I think I have dealt with an issue and addressed it, the issue comes back and slaps me up side the head. For me, that's just God's way of getting my attention and saying, "You, Meri, pay attention!"

There was one thing I did not realize until recently and that was that I harbored a belief that if my mother did not want me, maybe God did not either. When I say it now, I realize how absurd it sounds. Nevertheless, I was operating without even understanding why on that thought system.

If you remember, I talked about the piece of me that was set aside and would only let people get so close. I did not realize that I was doing this with God, as well. I did not even think to include God as a relationship that needed to be addressed. However, he loved me enough to remind me. That allowed me to move forward with a clean slate. That painful soul searching improved my spirituality. That is good news. I hope that my testimonial will give you hope if you, too, are struggling with your relationship with God.

Well, remember when I mentioned my need to create a connection or relationship after my parents died. There is another aspect to that and that is the importance of a physical structure called a home. I grew up in the same house my father built and mother lived in until she died. So growing up with an identified home structure was always there for me. Even if I moved around a lot, there would always be 3117 Foxianna Road for me to return to. It was always a place for me to visit while in college and a place for me to leave after college. It was my default address while in transition. I did not realize the importance of a physical structure and my emotional and psychological ties to that home until I sold the house and did not have it anymore. Why is it I always learn after the fact? Maybe one of these days I will get it right and "get it" before…. well, maybe in my next life.

That understanding really became evident during the first year of my marriage to Mike. It was the most difficult period since my parent's death. It was a wonder, Mike survived all the enlightenment I was acquiring. What I did not realize was how emotionally connected I was to the little things I had that belonged to my parents and what an important role a physical home plays in providing security and identity.

When I got married, I sold my house. I had just moved into that house about a year and a half before. I settled in and felt secure and comfortable and truly felt like it was my home more than any other house I had. Nevertheless, as I mentioned I sold it and moved into Mike's home, away from my friends that I had for fifteen years or more. This began setting off triggers. That filing cabinet was opening. Mike's house was much smaller than mine was and he was in the process of selling his house while we were building our home. Follow me so far? My personal things ended up in storage. And when we moved my things the only thing I could do was watch my personal items some of which I grew up looking at all my life get scratched, broken and shoved into a cold dark space of 10x12. It felt like a piece of me was being shoved into that cold dark space as well. I was living out of moving boxes for three months. Then Mike sold his house before our house was finished and we moved in with his mother for another three months. Now my moving box was reduced to a shoebox.

Those feelings of being lost and disconnected really came to the surface. It came out in anger and depression. (Some things never change.) The feelings were intense and I resorted back to my childhood. How could my husband do this to me? How could he put me in this situation by leaving me with nothing? He would try to reassure me and say I had him. However, I felt I could not rely on him because of the pain I was in. And I was thinking "yeah, right, you were the one who put me in this situation). He was not enough because he could always leave. (Fear of abandonment again.) I had lost myself once more.

Even though I had a husband who loved me and his family who had taken me in as there own. I still needed to be around something that was familiar and that I had history with, even if it was just an old desk that I used to play under as a child or a picture hanging on the wall of my family. I had no history with Mike and his family compared to my friends. I had a fifteen years plus relationship with my friends. This was extremely important because at that point in my life my friends were the only people on the face of the earth who knew me the longest since the death of my parents. My belongings such as furniture and pictures were my only other security. I was beginning to feel orphaned again. See a pattern here?

As you can see adoption can bring surprises to certain life events when you least expect it. Especially, when you think they are suppose to be exciting and positive circumstances. Well, the filing cabinet was not only opened but papers were thrown to the wind. Trying to explain this to someone was almost impossible and only added to my frustration. I cannot tell you how many times that I have said in the course of my conversations with Mike "you don't understand and you never will." It was not until we moved into our newly built home that I started to feel more rooted and secure. However, looking back at the situation I can truly say that my being uprooted was a trigger for that adoption filing cabinet to be reopened. It also brought to light how difficult and almost impossible it was for me to trust the fact that someone was going to take care of me and look out for my best interests. You see my thought pattern went as follows: if I had all my personal things around me that meant I was in control of my life. I felt I lost control and if I lost control that meant I couldn't take care of myself and that would be the end of my world as I knew it. Which I might add is not necessarily a bad thing; the world as I knew it that is. It is just extremely difficult to let go of old patterns.

The intensity again of the feelings I was experiencing was very high. It was a deep soulful pain coupled with fear and panic. When placed in that situation I immediately went back to the feelings of loneliness of being an orphan with no home and nothing that was mine. It was all community property. I think you can see just how important history is to a person. Not only can history create the reoccurrence of painful feelings but I can tell you my history was the corner stone to my security and identity. I truly believe it is even more important for children that are adopted to have that sense of history and connectivity. As I write this I found it extremely difficult to find the words that really convey what it was all like. I believe history is an aspect that others can take for granted. I know everyone has a history but not everyone has a history of connection to individuals from the beginning. Just by the fact you are adopted means that the history that connects you to the world has already been disrupted.

That is what I meant when I said to Mike "you don't understand and you never will." Mike was in his old stomping grounds where he grew up and went to school. He had a strong connection to the community and sense of identity to that community. It is a small country town where everyone knows everyone. Therefore, even if he lost his parents, changed jobs, churches, or added family like me he still had a sister, nephew, and a community that recognized and accepted him as belonging to that community. Mike grew up with familiar customs, smells, and activities in this community. I did not and never will have that in the community I am in now. And, that is why I think it is so important to have a sibling so that you can have a history and connection with at least one other person in the world that is unique to only you. However, that is another chapter.

So, that is why it was essential to my emotional well-being to have my family pictures up on my wall and to have my parent's things sitting out. There is one other thing in my life that is extremely important to me, that is my dancing. I think it is because again, it is something my parents encouraged when I was growing up. They recognized my natural talent. It was something I personally identified with. It built my self-esteem. It was something I always excelled at and I identified with as a part of me. It helps me keep centered and reconnected to my childhood and still today helps me maintain my self-esteem. It is something that is personal and mine that no one can take away. It grounds me. Ask me if I want to dance and my eyes light up! There is something spiritual for me about dancing, as well. As long as I can have some personal items and my ability to dance, I will not lose who I am.

There is a greater lesson and important perspective to understand in all this. That this brings to light that adopted children have a sense of what it either was like or could have been like if they did not have the family they have today. They have a keen awareness of the uncertainty in life that other people or children do not even give any thought to. That there are no guarantees in life and that by the throw of the heavenly dice things can change in an instant. Persons adopted have this perspective because they have lived it to some degree. It is inherent in the very fact they are adopted. So because of this it is important to have a detailed love story for your children and help them cultivate whatever talents they have. It will help anchor them in their life.

I think all these experiences have helped me to understand the importance of continuing to bond and connect to either people or things associated with me personally and that have a history with me. Adoption can bring this to light and that is not a bad thing because it brings us back to our beginnings and see the value of being connected to others. I know I have said it is difficult and there is a small piece of me that remains separate. However, I can say that small piece of me has gotten smaller and smaller as I continue to make good life choices. That is a good thing.

Even though connecting with others is a good thing, it is difficult in a world that reveres the Internet, cell phone and reality TV. With that being said, what continues to stand-alone is the need to have something that belongs only to you and to have a history that is all your own. That also is what the rituals offer—an understanding of your history, and gifts of a committed loving upbringing. That is something no one can take away from you.

Life is just a mirror, and what you see out there,
you must first see inside of you.

Wally "Famous" Amos

Chapter 7
Life From All Sides

I have already touched on what it was like growing up knowing I was adopted and the influence it had in my adult life. However, what I found interesting is that I am still making emotional connections and having experiences that are giving me the chance to resolve old issues that I did not even know were issues. I am not talking about the stuff I mentioned in previous chapters. What I am talking about are experiences that occurred while I was in the orphanage.

You probably wonder how that could have affected me since I was only twenty-one months old when I was adopted. I do not have cognitive memories but I can tell you I have feelings. One of the things we learn, as a therapist, is that experiences happening during the pre-verbal stage have an impact on the person and can resurface at any point in their lives. You can also acquire what they call body memories; that is when you experience an emotional or physical reaction in adulthood about an event that occurred when you were a child. It is usually triggered by what appears to be at the time an unrelated experience. Notice I said at the time appears unrelated. What you will find is that there is a connection once you start looking. A trigger might be when your own child becomes the age you were when you experienced the trauma or event. This can happen from a positive perspective as well. How many times have you heard an old tune and it took you right back where you were when you first heard it? You remember everything about that moment; you can even smell the old familiar smells. Well this can happen with other events as well. Allow me to give you an example. Keep in mind I lived in an orphanage in Europe from birth to twenty-one months.

Mike and I were at a restaurant. Cade was approximately four months old and we had finished dinner and I was looking at the dessert list. Mike had said, "You don't want to get dessert," and went into all the reasons why I shouldn't. I found myself getting enraged and even fearful inside. I had no idea what I was fearful or enraged about. (Note I used the word "rage", not angry. This is not a mistake nor would the word angry describe my feelings adequately. There is a difference and it is that difference that lets you know that there is a teaching moment ahead.) I found myself consumed with rage and fear even though I didn't say anything to Mike at the time. I have come to learn to keep my mouth shut and just ride out the emotion until I can figure it all out. Of course I learned that the hard way as well. Well anyway, I got home and it wasn't until the next evening as I was lying in bed still angry that Mike asked if something was wrong. Well that was the door I needed and I said to Mike very suddenly as if someone else was using my mouth to speak, "You don't understand. The only time anyone ever touched me was to feed me and now you want to take that away from me too." I am quoting this because it was, and still is, engraved in my brain.

Then this overwhelming sadness and loneliness came over me. I was surprised at what I just said. It was not something that was pre-thought out. I did not have a clue what was going on and Mike was looking at me strangely. However, it was at that point I realized I had tapped into experiences relating to the orphanage. I probably was the same age as Cade when I had that awareness and feeling. You see, experiences (feelings) have a way of making themselves at home in your body until they have a vehicle for expression. At an early age I may have realized that food meant attention and attention meant someone was going to touch me maybe for the first or second time that day. The feelings of sadness that there was not someone to be with me came out along with all the pent up loneliness. This sadness and loneliness was not about my present feelings, but rather an old feeling I actually had as a child. I just had no way of expressing them or anyone to express them too.

Understanding where my feelings of rage and fear were coming from, it made perfect sense. I was tapping into the fear of not being fed or touched and enraged that someone was trying to take the little comfort I did get away from me. After I was able to articulate these feelings, the sadness and loneliness lasted for about a half an hour and was replaced with immense relief. I felt like a weight was lifted from my shoulders both mentally and physically. I actually lost ten pounds over the next two weeks without even trying. It is amazing stuff! There are books written just on this phenomenon, which I find exciting. It also may be important to mention that I have struggled with my weight throughout my childhood. I still emotionally eat when things get real stressful.

When Cade turned eighteen months, I waited for the twenty-one-month mark to see what would happen then. If you think because you adopting a child as an infant or toddler that there will be no issues I am here to tell you that you're **wrong**! My experiences prove that. Especially for an international adoption where children are traditionally placed in orphanages and physical interaction is limited and sporadic at best.

So we have Cade home, now what? As they say, it's not over till the fat lady sings and believe me, she's still napping at our house. This is where the work begins for us adults who were adopted ourselves and have adopted. We are going through it all over again only from a different set of eyes and experience. What I find so wonderful about this is the amount of healing that has occurred during this process of adoption and will continue to occur through out Cade's development. It is a rather unique place to be. It is almost like standing in a clear glass octagon room where you can actually see and feel all sides of the adoption. I have been able to gain better perspective on what it was like for my mother and father to go through the adoption process, the birth mother's perspective and to relive some of my own adoption experiences as a child that I never had an opportunity to experience before. Being able to actually process some of your own adoption feelings can be a very powerful and painful experience. However, these experiences always bring value not only to your life but those closest to you. It has made me stronger and wiser so far gaining inherent strength and wisdom I can pass down to Cade. Is it not every parent's dream to give to their children what they did not have? Well now it can become a reality.

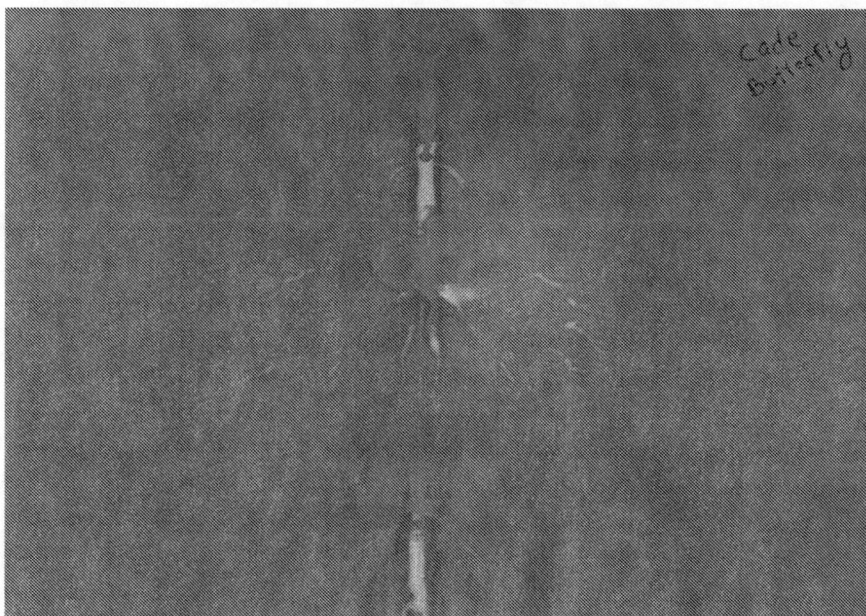

There is . . . nothing to suggest that mothering cannot be shared by several people.

H. R. Schaffer

Chapter 8
Mother to Mother

Here is where I sing the praises (again) of knowing as much about your birth mother or father as you can and meeting her or him if possible. In my situation, it was invaluable. Each time I received a letter from her for Cade it gave me insight into the pain and struggle that went through her mind. Even when the birth mother knows she is making the right decision it still is a very emotional and painful process. This is the very reason you need to work with an adoption agency that can provide you with information but also supports the birth mother in going through with the adoption.

Mike and I were very lucky because even with support and counseling offered to Monica, she could have changed her mind. But Monica didn't do that and I think counseling and continued support throughout the process really made a difference. Getting to meet and know Monica allowed me to understand a little more about my own birth mother. I was able to pick out the similarities and realize this decision is something both sides live with for the rest of their lives. For the birth mother it is not something you can erase and, for the adopted child, it is something that will become an integral part of their lives. Adopted parents will have to address it with their children some day. Knowing all this offered me a time to heal a part of me that I thought I dealt with. As a child and still today as an adult I wish I knew what it was like for my birth mother to place me for adoption. As a child, I remember hoping that it was difficult and that my birth mother struggled with having to give me up. I know that may sound awful but wishing that she struggled was my way of adding value and purpose to my life. That thought offered me comfort some how.

Having experienced first hand what Monica had gone through actually solidified that wish and made it a reality for me. I believe many people think that birth mothers are taking the easy way out and do not have to deal with anything after they walk away. However, based on an individual's circumstance each person's experience will be different. But no matter how easy it may appear on the outside or how they may say they are not affected there will always be a part of them that will be forever changed whether they admit it or not. Again just one more reason to make sure there is support and counseling for the birth mother. The value of being able to see and understand Monica's experience allowed me to take the sting out of my anger. It allowed me the opportunity to actually gain respect and love for the woman who I knew so little about but loved me enough to go through all she had to so I could have a better life. Even though I thought that in my head, it finally made it to my heart after meeting Cade's birthmother (thanks, Monica).

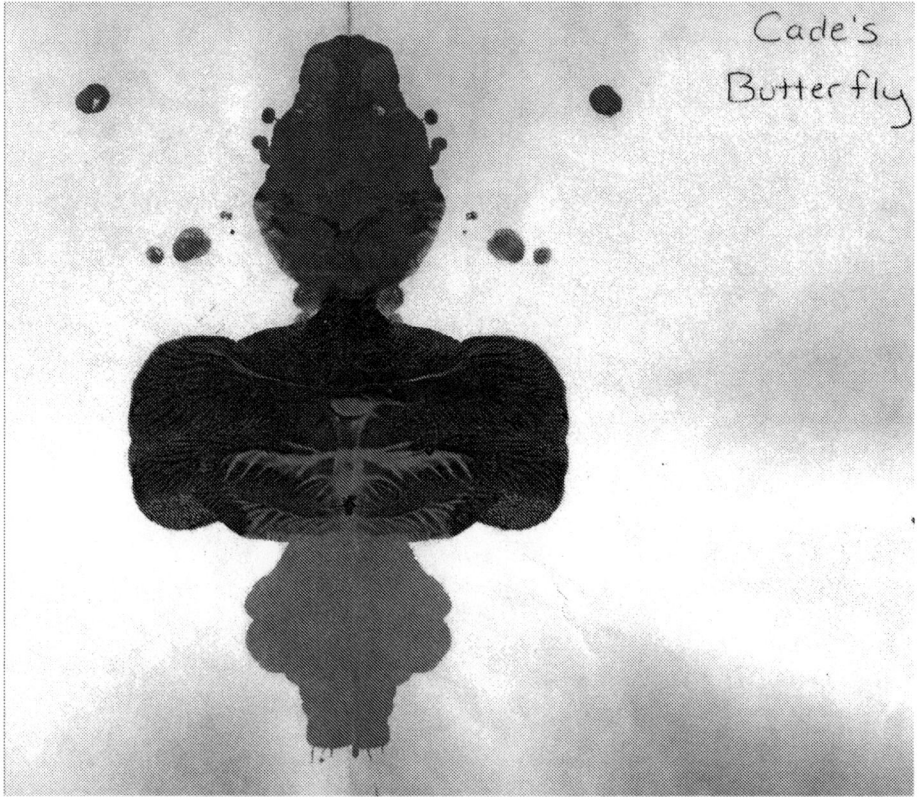

As the family goes, so goes the nation and so goes the
whole world in which we live.

Pope John Paul II

Chapter 9
The Great Teacher
Parenthood

nfortunately, my mother and father did not leave me a diary as to what it was like for them to go through the adoption process other than what they shared with me over the years. That is why I feel strongly about having something in writing. There is something powerful about the written word especially when there is someone around to reinforce it by telling you the story.

When I was being disciplined as a young pre-teen (I was probably about twelve), I would think in the back of my mind "you wouldn't be doing this if I wasn't adopted; you wouldn't be treating me this way." (It's not fair, sound familiar. Get use to it. It is the common mantra for teenagers and some adults.) I also remember being in conflict constantly thinking that I must be good or they might want to put me back but yet being rebellious so that if they were going to send me back, they would do it soon and get it over with. Now how much sense does that make? To a young, pre-teen girl it makes perfect sense. I remember thinking that quite often. I guess I figured if they could get me that easy they could send me back just as easy.

This is where understanding the process helps as well. It is not that easy to go through the process. And, there is a lot of thought and preparation that goes into adopting children. My behavior continued into adulthood where I worked hard at always making them proud of me. It was not so much that they would send me back but more they would reject me somehow. *(Please note that all these thoughts that were going through my mind were never discussed with my parents. I kept it to myself.)* My parents never did anything that would let me believe that they had any intentions of sending me back or rejecting me. In fact, they constantly told me they loved me and that having me in their lives made them so happy. It was just my own thoughts.

But the true understanding came when I had the opportunity to be placed in my parent's shoes. I came to realize they gave me many gifts, talents, and teachings that have made me who I am. I refuse to say the old adage that they parented me the best way they could with the information they had at the time. That reeks of a cop out. What I hope to do is to give Cade what my parents gave me and so much more.

There was this awareness of how I felt when I first laid eyes on Cade and how there was and is no distinction in my mind, my heart, or soul about him being our child. Therefore, I will discipline him as my parents disciplined me out of love and wanting me to be someone with values, morals, and sense of responsibility. I hope I can be as successful with Cade as they were with me.

There are also similarities between my parents and Mike and I. (What goes around comes around holds true here in my case.) We both were older parents, my adoptive mother was infertile, and both agreed adoption was an option. It gave me insight into my parents that I did not have before. It allowed me to see them more as people who struggled with their own issues of wanting children, paying for adoption, filling out the paperwork, waiting and waiting some more then finally having a child to bring home. It gave me a chance to put to rest any doubt in my mind about the feelings my parents had for me. What I also noticed were the things that were important to me over the years. Growing up I remember it really made me feel good when someone said you must be Alex's or Edna's daughter or you must be a Dimoff. Today I love it when someone says "your son, Cade" or "there's Cade's mommy." Whatever is said after that is just icing on the cake even if it is bad news. By the way, when he does something good he is my son when he does something bad he is Mike's son. Isn't that how it works? The important thing is either way he is our son.

Now that I am older it is important for me to see the similarity between my parents' personality characteristics and my own. I find it exciting that I am much like my father: strong-minded, decisive, risk taking, valuing and honoring hard work. I initially found this odd since we seemed to be always fighting. But you put two bulls in a closet and see what happens! It is difficult to have two hardheaded, decisive people under the same roof. Trust me. I am sure at times my mom was ready to ship us both back to Kentucky to learn a little southern grace.

However, I also was able to discover similarities with my mother, she was humble, but had a graceful, quiet strength and a gentle spirit about her and I believe I got my intuitiveness and compassion and dedication to family from her. There was one message my mother made a point to share with me before she died. It is not earth shattering or extremely profound in nature. It was just my mom and the vision from which she operated her life.

She made a point to sit me down about six months after my father died and told me the following: I may not be around for when you get married so I want to give you some advice. She started with I am not college educated as you are and I am glad and very proud of you graduating. But there are just some things that college can't teach you that life and death can. And since I have forty some years of life more than you do I hope you will listen to what I have to say. She went on to say...when you get married I want you to do two things everyday without fail. And they must be done in this order without exception. Now she had me really thinking what she was going to tell me. She went on to say I want you to promise me that every night before you head hits the pillow you do these two things and if you do them I know you will be taken care and your life will be full and rich in blessings. Now here they are: You *first* must thank God for all that you have including your husband even if you are mad at him and most of the time you will be. (How did she know?) *Secondly*, tell your husband and children that you love them even if you may not feel that way at the moment. Then once you have children teach them to do the same. Only then when you have committed yourself to doing that daily for the rest of your life will you have your priorities and vision for your life in order. The rest will fall into place.

How simple yet how wise. You see that was her vision and it was that vision that kept her alive as long as she was. Her life was filled with sickness. During my childhood, I remember her being in and out of the hospital with cancer, heart disease, diabetes, gall bladder. (You name it she has had it.) I remember when I was about fourteen, watching her walk out of the recovery room after surgery to meet us. I remember being so amazed at the time. She used to always tell me that it was her love for Dad and me that kept her going and her desire and commitment to raise me. I learned about long-suffering with dignity and grace from my mother. She taught me the meaning and value of adversity and how it can refine us to become more Christ-like. What great gifts and advice she gave me.

I only discovered these great lessons after she died. As mentioned earlier I was always a little behind on things and this was no exception. All of this is important because this is what will become part of Cade's story and I will be passing these traits on to him, I hope. It is important for him to understand where they came from. I just pray that Cade is not as old as I was before he finds the value of it all and I hope I am alive to see it.

Whatever God's dream about man may be, it seems certain it cannot come true unless man cooperates.

Stella Terrill Mann

Chapter 10
The Radio Caller

This is a chapter that I did not know I was going to add. But because I had such strong feelings about it, I thought I would share it with you. I think you will see how it ties in with the message from this book.

I was somewhat disturbed about a conversation I had with a friend some time ago. She was telling me that she had listened to a radio program that had aired a talk segment on adoption. *(Now please note: I am responding to my friend's interpretation of the program. I also do not believe addressing personal issues on the radio is a healthy avenue to take.)*

The conversation went something like this:
My friend stated that a lady had called in and was sharing with the listening audience how she tried to have children but couldn't. She and her husband decided to adopt approximately three years ago.
The children ranged from infant to four years of age. She adopted all three at one time because she did not want to separate the siblings. The caller spoke about how distressed she was over how she did not feel connected to the children and was not able to bond with them. She was thinking about going back to work as a solution to her problem and that she did not know what she was going to do with them. The conversation with my friend was enough to start my blood pressure to rise.

Maybe I should start by saying that I am sure this woman's heart was in the right place when she adopted these beautiful children. But *my* disclaimer—remember, *Life According to Meri?*—is this: It brings to life some real issues and makes the points I have tried to reiterate in this book. Life gets played out in different scenarios. With that said here I go . . .

I will start with the most important fact and that is... it is the adult's responsibility to bond with the children they adopt. By the sheer definition of adult, it is our responsibility to understand perfectly why we are adopting and to remain committed for the long haul. Maybe that is a hard-nosed approach to a delicate situation but we are talking about children's lives here. And most of the time we are talking about children that have been abandoned and abused. Why add to the trauma just because we have acted irresponsibly by making a knee jerk or emotional decision? This is a prime example of what can happen when you do not honestly address why you are adopting and are not willing to take responsibility to confront your own issues. I certainly do not know this woman or all her circumstances. I admire her courage to adopt all three children at once. I know how hard it is to keep up with one. But if three years have gone by and you are at the point of calling into a radio show and verbalize this to the world, I can only guess that those children are hearing that message loud and clear on a daily basis. Do you think they wonder how wanted they are and emotionally committed their mother is to them? Now, she is wondering what to do with them!! What kind of statement is that? What, she got them during a Blue Light Special at Kmart and wants to return them? Did they come with a money-back guarantee? Sorry for the sarcasm here but I believe it was warranted.

From what my friend said, the radio show did not help matters either. The response was supposedly, "I am so sorry for you." Now that is wonderful but what about the children who are listening to their mother cry on the air about how she does not feel bonded to them? How do you think they feel? Believe me if they were not in the room at the time they will find out about it. People love to pass along gossip that hurts. Can you image going to school the day after that airing? According to my friend, the topic of how the children were affected was not even discussed. The conversation revolved around the mother's feelings and not how the children must feel. Well let me tell you (can you tell I'm fired up by now?) if she was talking about her biological children that way I bet that would not have been the response she received. I bet you someone would have called in or the station would have said a few choice words and told her she had a serious problem and to get some help. They would have shown compassion for the children. How is it possible that a mother cannot bond with her biological children? Seems unnatural does it not? But, and this is a big but, because the children we are speaking about are adopted, the response is, "Oh, I am so sorry for you!"

I have heard the term disposable children used when speaking of adopted children. I find the word deplorable and can only pray it is not accurate. Is that how we as a society think of adopted children? If so, there is a major problem. It's this second-class citizen mentality that infuriates me. It tells me that it is the adult's perspective that adopted children are suppose to be grateful that "we" adopted them and it is our expectation that they make our life whole and pleasant. And do so out of the gratitude. After all, we took them out of the "hell" they were in or could have been in. And if the adoptive parents haven't bonded with them there must be something wrong with the kids. How insane does that sound to you? Nevertheless, some adults operate out of that belief whether they know it or not. For some it is an unconscious thought for the most part. But remember how our emotions and intent reveal themselves in our behavior. Listen to how loudly this radio caller's behavior speaks—since I haven't bonded with them I will go back to work so I don't have to spend that much time with them and remind myself of my situation.

Please do not get me wrong about being a working mother. I am a working mother. My children go to a Christian day care and preschool in which I am actively involved. I believe you can work and still love and connect with your children at the same time. Cade and I are proof of that. We are very bonded to each other. Again, the motivion and intent is the key to everything. It is the intent that is reflected in our behavior and then passed on to our children. Children are very intuitive. They know the difference between mommy leaving to go to work and being loved and mommy going to work to get away from them because they do not know what else to do. Think about it! Wouldn't you? Why should children be any different?

I mentioned about a hundred times before if we do not work out our own issues first then we will make decisions from those emotions. How devastating can it be not only to you but the children as well? You must be honest as to why you are adopting, find out and make sure you know what your expectations are and again be honest about them. If you are adopting because you want someone to fill an emotional hole that you hae because of either unresolved infertility issues or past and/or present emotional or physical abuse, or you're in a failing marriage then **stop**! Children are children whether they are biologically yours or adopted. They will cry, they will test you, they will love you one minute and hate you the next. They will tell you that you are the meanest person alive when you tell them no. If you are not emotionally prepared for this and your expectations are self centered and unrealistic there is only heartache for everyone involved ahead of you.

This radio caller is a prime example of not being emotionally prepared. Please do not let yourself get to that point. Get help. I am not saying that there will never be a time that you won't second-guess yourself about your decision to adopt or that emotional triggers won't traumatize you. I can guarantee it will happen. That's life. What I am stressing here is that the adult in us must be willing to challenge and confront those issues as they come up and work through them. We have to see that as our responsibility and commitment and our responsibility and commitment alone—not that of our children. It must be our responsibility as a parent *for the children* because it will ultimately make you and your children closer.

You can do this as a family, by yourself, with a therapist, or a guru—just make sure you do it. It needs to be done so you can freely move on and continue to have the capacity to love your children, as they inherently have the right to be loved. *(Note: I did not say love your children as your own—for some reason I don't like that phrase. The statement itself implies a differentiation that they are not your children.)* I use the word "your children" because when you adopt you make claim to these children *and* they are your own. How they got to you is immaterial. And that brings me to my final topic.

Our lives improve only when we make changes—and the first and most difficult risk we take is to be honest with each other.

Walter Anderson

Chapter 11
Someone Else's Child

I'm not sure what to say in this chapter. Can you believe it? Me at a loss for words! I feel compelled to bring up the issue that some people cannot or do not want to raise or love someone else's child. To me, this is such a foreign concept. Nevertheless, I recognize that some people feel this way and therefore feel obligated to address this issue.

I am not going to label this type of mentality as gender based because I do not have statistics to support that. I also do not want to come across as judgmental. I just want to share some of my ideas and leave it at that.

I have come across a few couples where one is in tears because the other partner could not accept a child that was not of "their blood".

All I can say to that is please consider the following information. Remember when I shared with you my initial response on hearing about Cade's birth mother and her situation and how arrogant I was? This ties into that initial response and puts a perspective on what Mike and I went through in deciding about Cade. What I am about to share with you are some struggles and fears that we had to confront and deal with. If we had not it would have ultimately kept us from accepting Cade—which brings me physical, emotional and psychological pain just thinking about it.

What I find interesting is that I always thought of myself as open minded, non-discriminatory, and painfully non-prejudiced in the way I look at the world. In fact, I used to pride myself in that. Well, pride can only take you to that place where you get your back pushed up against the wall and your knees knocked out from under you. It is when you cannot back up anymore that you are forced to take an honest look at your beliefs and fears. That is what happened with us.

When Cade was first presented to us as an option we only knew the mother. The father was unknown. He could be Caucasian, Hispanic, Oriental or African American. There was a good chance he would be Bi-racial and we were to make a decision based on the information we had at the present. At first, we thought we were getting pushed into making a decision. I have to say that it was the best thing that could have happen to us. Of course, we did not know that at the moment but we soon came to understand it. What it forced us to do was to evaluate our true morals, ethical beliefs, and confront any prejudices we had and ones we did not know we had. When you start thinking in terms of a forever family that throws a much brighter light on all your ugly spots. You know what I mean by ugly spots— arrogance, prejudice, and most commonly, fear. The ones we have been able to cover up with the make up of self-righteousness rhetoric . . . until now. My husband, as wonderful as he may be, is the total opposite of me. He is very concrete and, in his own self-described terms, practical. He is the person that wants to see, feel, touch, and smell things and know all the facts before he makes a decision. So this was very difficult for him. I also have to admit that I was thinking about whether I could bond and accept this child no matter the race, physical condition, or appearance? I did not like even having that question in my mind. Let alone not having a confident answer. But by being pushed into facing and making that decision it forced us to rely on something much greater than the facts and that was faith.

We started to look at how this opportunity presented itself and exactly what we were being offered here and all of a sudden all the unknowns really did not make a difference. And it was all because we could see the hand of God working. All the arrogance in the world is no match for God. It was only then that we truly felt relief and could come to the place that we did. And that place was no matter who his father was and what the circumstances were around his conception we were committed to love him.

It was at that very point that we were able to begin to love him for just being. Is that not a wonderful thought? Do we not all aspire and want to be loved just for being? Isn't that an inherent right of all human beings? He was loved by God first and is God's child first and definitely ours second. From that point on everything went like clock work. (Go figure!)

What I am saying is if you are struggling with the concept of loving someone else's child I would begin to ask yourself some questions. Like what are your fears about raising another's child? What is truly important in your life? If it is the unknown family history or shaky circumstances, then ask yourself if you can be sure your biological child would be free of physical afflictions or mental health disorders? If you wonder which is more powerful and will have more influence in the child—nature or nurture, I know there are studies out there that can defend each position. However, I can tell you that there is something even more powerful than nature or nurture combined and that is love. I am living proof that we grow to become what we live.

I told you what I have learned from my parents and the characteristics I have acquired and attributed to my mother and father. I just know if my parents could not have raised someone else's child not only would I not be able to write this book but also I wouldn't be alive today. I would have been the ones left behind buried under the orphanage rubble and forgotten. Therefore, if you want to work through that struggle I encourage you to find a good counselor who can help you through it. Believe me, it is all worth it in the end. This principle also applies to raising ethnic children as well. Can you love a child who does not look like you? Or did not come from a pristine family background? Is there anyone who has? If not, why? Then are you willing to challenge those feelings? Because if you are not willing, you may lose out on the most beautiful opportunity of a lifetime and, worse yet, make a decision that you are unprepared to make. You will do a disservice to both you and the child. Because whatever child you decide to adopt you must be able to love unconditionally and be willing to go to the ends of the earth for. Because that is what they deserve and that is what parents do.

Have I preached enough yet on this topic? I guess you can tell this is another sensitive area where I have strong opinions. And again please remember they are just that my opinions—just food for thought to keep in your backpack while you travel through life, and hopefully, through adoption.

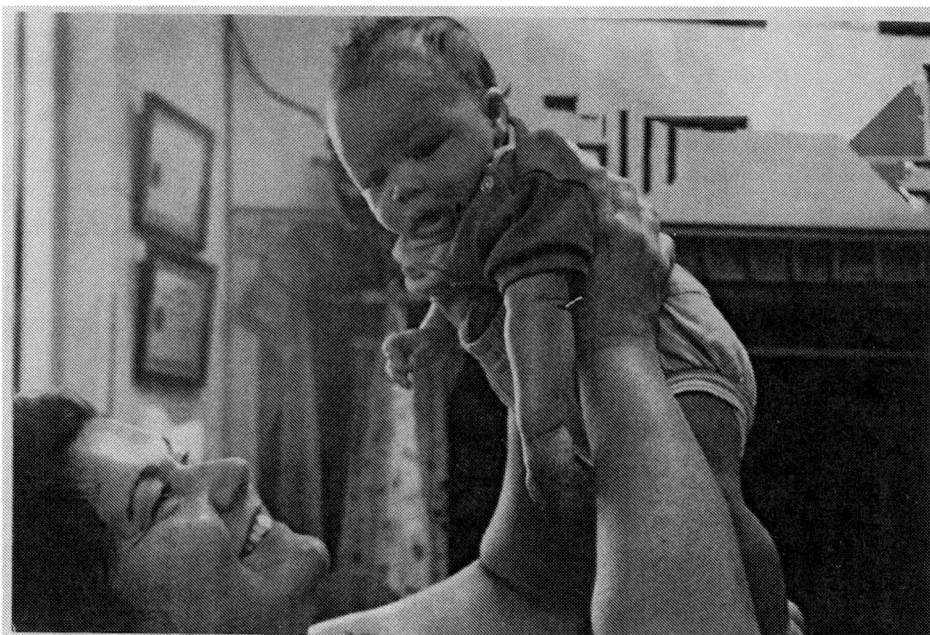

Here's a test to find whether your mission on earth is finished:
If you're alive, it isn't.

Richard Bach

Chapter 13
It's Not Over...I'm Still Alive

Well, that is pretty much Cade's and my story. The pages of life continue to be written and I am happy to say Cade is turning into a fine young man. My goal will remain consistent and that is to continue to grow and to learn from him and in turn to teach him what I have learned so he will have a love story for his children—and his children's children.

We have recently adopted a sister for Cade so another book or two is in the making. Her name is Jana Mari. Please look for her book, which I am heartbroken to say, is a completely different experience.

In the Absence of Love: Jana's Story will explore yet another adventure in adoption.

Also please use the journal in the back of this book. It may help you in whatever decision-making stage you may be in, or help you in writing your own love story. May all your lives be filled with the joyous noise of children and may you experience one of the greatest gifts of all--*Life!*

Epilogue

I hope you enjoyed the book. Life always offers up so much more than we expect so that's never all there is. Over the next few pages, you will read excerpts from my up coming book, **In the Absence of Love, Jana's Story**. This book will take you on another new journey through the emotional and psychological maze of adoption where you will find yourself in the throes of a battle for life itself. I will warn you now it is not a warm and fuzzy, feel-good book. The book is not designed that way; life is not designed that way. It is being written out of love for children and confronts the fabric of our nation's view of children and hopefully challenges each reader's own thoughts about children not only in the reader's personal life, but professional life as well. So caseworkers, attorneys, judges, foster care parents, biological parents read with caution and an open mind.

We all know what love is when we see and feel it. Books have been dedicated to the topic and songs written about it. The Bible gives us a clear description of what love is and romantic novels allow us to fantasize about it. But, how do we know when love is not present? And when it isn't present, how does the absence of love affect our children? I know that may sound like a simple question. We can describe it as all kinds of examples of abuse or trauma. But do we really understand the depth and insidiousness of the absence of love in our daily lives and in our daily lives of our children?

In the Absence of Love: Jana's Story
Below are just some excerpts of what happens to children when love is absent from their lives…

Chapter 2:
In the absence of love there is fear: What else could there be? If we believe there is no such thing as love, or that no one loves me or, the worst fear of all, that I am unlovable, then I have everything and everyone to fear. It then becomes a matter of self-preservation and survival of the fittest. How often do we see this played out in our childcare system where children have been placed in multiple homes? The fear of reaching out has become too great. What was once an innocent and unquestionable belief that I am lovable and someone loves me has been replaced by fear that no one loves me and that the person with me will leave me. Then comes the belief that love is not real and does not exist because there is nothing constant in their lives to show love. How can you believe in something that is eternal and all encompassing when your life has modeled only the opposite?

In the absence of love there is anger: Once the fear subsides and the children's' defenses become stronger, then the anger arrives. This becomes displayed in statements like, "I don't need anyone," "I can take care of myself." The anger can become so consuming that it becomes the child's world. Any offering of love, which can open the child's world, sometimes has the opposite effects at this stage. They emotional shut down and the child lives in darkness. This dark world is a place in which the child becomes ever vigilant and skeptical as a defense mechanism against hurt. Anger allows them to distance themselves from the world. It is their protection from others and what they believe as impending doom.

In the absence of love there is judgment: This is where right and wrong take on a whole new meaning. Actually where there is fear and anger there is only wrong, which, of course, makes perfect sense. If you are not shown love then there must be something wrong with you. Judgment begins the day you were born.

The longer the system keeps them; the longer they are placed in non-permanent homes, the louder this message is heard: My parents don't love me, the people who take care of me don't love me, and since the system doesn't let me be loved, there is something wrong with me.

Chapter 7
A Mother's Plea; A Child's Plea

This chapter is for all of you who work for children. (Note: I said work *for*, not with, children.) There is a definite difference, you know. Yes, *you*, Judge. Yes, *you*, Lawyer. Yes, *you*, caseworkers, social workers, and counselors. But especially, *you*, Politician. All of you have an affect on the emotional, psychological, physical, and spiritual health of our children who are our future.

Know that every decision, every word out of your mouth, every bias and preconceived notion, every action made in relation to a child will be forever embedded in their minds and in their hearts. These are children *you* are responsible for. **Yes, responsible for.** I say that because it is what I believe to be the crucial missing element when it comes to our children. Children get lost in the process, politics, and paperwork because they are not considered as important. The process, politics and paperwork take priority.

I believe that those individuals who are key decision makers have lost or never have found the personal sense of responsibility for these children, plus the accountability factor to hold people responsible seems to have been lost as well. Accountable for what, you may ask? Accountable for the feelings these children have—feelings of anger, hopelessness, fear of trust and love, and feelings of loneliness. Loneliness created by these children being allowed to languish in systems, temporary homes, abusive family systems—all because paperwork has not been completed or the abuse has not reached egregious proportions.

I know this sound harsh, but I believe the system has been harsh to our children. Although there are some who do not fall into this category, they are the exception and not the norm.

Journal

Use these pages to write your souls desire and may you discover your own love story.

Happy Journaling!

We don't receive wisdom, we must discover it for ourselves after a journey that no one can take for us or spare us.

Marcel Proust

What wisdom have you obtained from your life journey that is closest to your heart?

If you cannot get rid of the family skeleton, you may as well make it dance.

George Bernard Shaw

What family skeletons are in your closet?

The only cure for grief is action.

George Henry Lewis

What action have you taken to resolve your grief? And would you do it again or choose to do it differently next time?

Life engenders life. Energy creates energy. It is by spending oneself that one becomes rich.

Sara Bernhardt

Where do you currently spend yourself now and where would you like to spend more of yourself in the future?

Love is everything it's cracked up to be . . .
It really is worth fighting for, being brave for, risking
everything for.

Erica Jong

When in your life were you the bravest and what were you willing to fight for and risk everything for?

Life is a mirror, and what you see out there, you must first see inside you.

Wally "Famous" Amos

Look in the mirror and describe the person that you see. Are you what you expected?

Our lives improve only when we take chances—and the first and most difficult risk we take is that we be honest with ourselves.

Walter Anderson

What is the biggest lie you ever told yourself? Are you still living that lie today?

There is . . . nothing to suggest that mothering cannot be shared by several people.

H.R. Schaffer

What is your definition of family and what is your definition of father . . . mother?

Here is a test to find whether your mission on earth is finished: If you're alive, it isn't.

Richard Bach

What do you believe is your mission on earth and are you living it?

I believe in looking reality straight in the eye and denying it.

Garrison Keillor

What has been staring you in the eye that you have denied all these years?

Whatever God's dream about man may be, it seems certain it cannot come true unless man cooperates.

Stella Terrill Mann

What have you been dragging your feet about that you know you should be doing?

As the family goes, so goes the nation and so goes the whole world in which we live.

Pope John Paul II

What do you want for your family and how will you make sure that they get it?

Printed in the United States
94692LV00004B/422/A